PLATE TECTONICS

EARTH'S MOVING CRUST

BY DARLENE R. STILLE

Content Advisers: Roger Larson, Professor, Graduate School of
Oceanography, University of Rhode Island, Narragansett
Bryce Hoppie, Associate Professor of Geology,
Minnesota State University, Mankato

Science Adviser: Terrence E. Young Jr., M.Ed., M.L.S.,
Jefferson Parish (Louisiana) Public School System

Reading Adviser: Rosemary G. Palmer, Ph.D., Department of Literacy,
College of Education, Boise State University

PLATE TECTONICS

Compass Point Books • 3109 West 50th Street, #115 • Minneapolis, MN 55410

Visit Compass Point Books on the Internet at *www.compasspointbooks.com*
or e-mail your request to *custserv@compasspointbooks.com*

Photographs ©: Tom Bean/Corbis, cover; Roger Ressmeyer, 4, 20, 33, 43; Digital Vision, 5, 25, 28; PhotoDisc, 8, 12, 30; Shutterstock/Michael Almond, 10; Brian A. Vikander/Corbis, 16; Olivier Matthys/EPA/Corbis, 17; Robert Yager/Getty Images, 22; Shehzad Noorani/Peter Arnold, 24; Gary Braasch/Corbis, 27; Pierre Vauthey/Corbis, 31; Shutterstock/Keith Levit, 34; The Granger Collection, New York, 35; Bettmann/Corbis, 36; Ken Lucas/Visuals Unlimited, 37; Norbert Wu/Minden Pictures, 39; Scientifica/Visuals Unlimited, 40; SIO Archives/UCSD, 41; AFP/Getty Images, 44; Shutterstock/Dmitry Pichugin, 46.

Editor: Anthony Wacholtz
Designer/Page Production: The Design Lab
Photo Researchers: Lori Bye and Marcie C. Spence
Cartographer: XNR Productions, Inc.
Illustrator: Eric Hoffmann

Art Director: Jaime Martens
Creative Director: Keith Griffin
Editorial Director: Carol Jones
Managing Editor: Catherine Neitge

Library of Congress Cataloging-in-Publication Data
   Plate tectonics : earth's moving crust / by Darlene R. Stille.
      p. cm. — (Exploring science)
Includes index.
   ISBN-13: 978-0-7565-1957-5 (hardcover)
   ISBN-10: 0-7565-1957-8 (hardcover)
   1. Plate tectonics—Juvenile literature. I. Title. II. Series.
   QE511.4.S735 2006
   551.1'36—dc22   2006006764

About the Author

Darlene R. Stille is a science writer and author of more than 80 books for young people. She grew up in Chicago and attended the University of Illinois, where she discovered her love of writing. She has received numerous awards for her work. She lives and writes in Michigan.

TABLE OF CONTENTS

Feeling the Earth Move

EARTH IS A RESTLESS PLANET. The ground that seems solid underfoot can suddenly begin to shake and heave with the violent force of an earthquake. Earthquakes can topple the brick walls of buildings and snap the steel and concrete spans of bridges as though they were made of matchsticks.

Wooden braces kept a house from completely collapsing after an earthquake in San Francisco in 1989.

A majestic snowcapped mountain stands silently above peaceful lakes and forests. Then suddenly, with a terrifying roar, the top blows off. Great clouds of ash may cover the sky. Rivers of red-hot molten rock may flow down the sides of a volcanic mountain, burning and burying everything in their paths.

A forest was set ablaze after the eruption of a nearby volcano.

Although the ground usually seems quiet and still, it is moving very slowly. Over millions of years, the movement in the lithosphere, Earth's crust and upper mantle, has changed oceans and continents. It has caused mountain ranges to appear and created chains of islands. This movement is the cause of earthquakes, volcanoes, and other wonders, such as fountains of boiling water called geysers. Earth's lithosphere can move because it is made up of gigantic plates of solid rock that slip and slide over hot, flowing rock beneath.

LAYERS OF EARTH

Like a baseball or an onion, planet Earth is made up of layers. The three main layers are the crust, the mantle, and the core. The layers grow hotter the deeper they extend down into the center of Earth.

The crust is the outermost layer of Earth and the thinnest of the three layers. Mountains, valleys, hills, and plains are all part of the crust. Lake bottoms and ocean floors are also part of Earth's crust. The crust that makes up dry land is thicker than the crust that makes up the ocean floor. Crust carrying mountain ranges can be up to 44 miles (70 kilometers) thick. The crust beneath the oceans is usually about 3 miles (5 km) thick.

Beneath the crust is a layer of rock called the mantle.

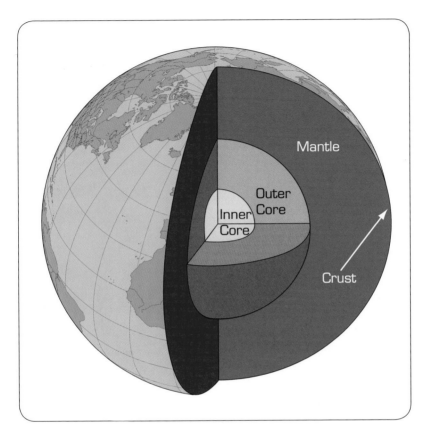

The mantle, which is about 1,800 miles (2,880 km) thick, is the largest layer of Earth. Rock in the mantle is very hot. The mantle rock close to the crust is about 1,300 degrees Fahrenheit (700 degrees Celsius). Near the core, mantle rock reaches temperatures of up to 7,200 F (4,000 C). Mantle rock that is above 2,900 F (1,600 C) partially melts and begins to flow slowly like very thick road tar. Rock above it that is cooler

and more dense falls downward as hotter rock rises, creating convection currents in the mantle that move heat like water boiling in a pot on the stove.

The upper part of the mantle and the thin rocky crust make up the solid lithosphere, which is the coolest part of Earth. The hot, nearly molten part of the mantle just below the lithosphere is called the asthenosphere. The lithosphere is broken up into gigantic solid plates, which move around on

Although Earth's interior does not boil like a heated pot of water, convection moves heat inside Earth in a similar way.

the flowing, nearly molten rock of the asthenosphere.

The innermost part of Earth, the core, is a very hot place, with temperatures ranging from 7,200 to 9,000 F (4,000 to 5,000 C). The core is made mainly of iron and nickel and has two parts. The outer core, which begins about 1,800 miles (2,880 km) below the surface, is liquid metal and can flow like pancake syrup. The inner core begins about 3,188 miles (5,100 km) below the surface. Even though the temperature in the inner core is very high, great pressure from the weight of the planet around it keeps the inner core solid.

GIGANTIC PLATES

The gigantic slabs of rock that make up Earth's lithosphere are called tectonic plates. Some of the plates carry continents, some carry oceans, and some carry a combination of both. The movements of these plates over time created all the features on Earth, from the highest mountains to the deepest seafloor. As the plates move, they can set off earthquakes, cause molten

DID YOU KNOW?

The word *tectonics* comes from a Greek word meaning "to build." Scientists chose the phrase *plate tectonics* to describe how the surface of Earth is "built" from plates of rock.

rock to spew out of volcanoes, give rise to islands, push up mountain ranges, and create new seas.

WHY EARTH IS HOT

What makes rock inside Earth hot enough to melt? Where does this heat come from?

Geologists believe the answer lies in the distant past, shortly after Earth was formed. Planetary scientists believe Earth and the other planets were formed from a cloud of dust

The massive peaks of the Pinnacles National Monument in California were formed from an ancient volcano, erosion, and tectonic movement.

and gas located around our sun about 4.5 billion years ago. Material in this cloud began to clump together, and these clumps began to spin. Gravity pulled more material toward one of the clumps until the early Earth began to take shape.

There were different kinds of chemical elements in the dust and gas cloud. Hydrogen and helium gas were the lightest elements. Iron, nickel, and other metals were the heaviest elements. There were also radioactive elements present in the cloud, which are unstable elements that decay and change into other elements. Under the force of gravity, the heavier elements began to sink toward the center of the forming Earth. At the same time, hunks of space rocks called asteroids and meteors, along with small comets, crashed into Earth's surface.

Geologists believe there were three possible ways in which heat was generated inside Earth. Some think gravitational energy changed to heat energy as the force of gravity pulled heavy materials toward the center of the planet. Others believe the energy of motion in speeding space rocks changed to heat energy when the rocks slammed into Earth. As a third possibility, heat could have been generated by the decay of radioactive elements.

Earth's interior became so hot that everything melted. The heaviest elements—iron and nickel—sank and formed the core. Lighter, rocky materials floated up to form the crust. The materials that were in between formed the mantle.

Although Earth has cooled off some since it formed, there is still plenty of heat in the interior. This heat keeps mantle rock hot enough to melt, allowing the plates to move slowly over long periods of time and to drive the processes that create volcanoes, hot springs, and geysers.

Craters are formed when meteorites crash into Earth. The collision of meteorites may have helped create the heat energy found in Earth.

Earth's Plates and How They Move

THERE ARE 14 large, irregularly shaped tectonic plates as wide as several thousand miles. There are also a number of smaller plates, which are only a few hundred miles wide.

Geologists have given the plates names. The largest plate is called the Pacific plate, which carries the Pacific Ocean. One of the smaller plates is the Juan de Fuca plate, along the northwest coast of North America. Geologists have also found very small plates about the size of medium to small U.S. states along the edges or boundaries of large plates. They call these small plates microplates.

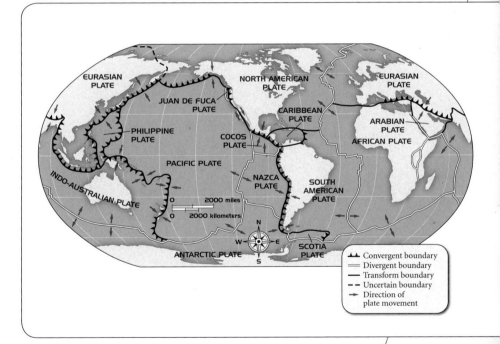

Earth's crust is divided into tectonic plates that are continuously moving.

PLATE MOVEMENTS

There are three basic ways tectonic plates move in relation to one another. They can move apart, crash together, or slide past one another. Geologists classify plate movements by the ways in which the plates move at their boundaries. There are three types of plate boundaries: divergent, convergent, and transform.

Divergent plate boundaries occur when two plates move away from each other. The North American and Eurasian plates are moving apart, splitting down the middle of the Atlantic Ocean floor. When two plates move apart, hot molten rock called magma can build up between the plates. One place where this is happening is called the Mid-Atlantic Ridge. The ridge is an undersea mountain range that started forming when magma rose and cooled to form a new crust at the edge of the spreading plates.

Plates moving apart have also formed other features on Earth, such as the spectacular Great Rift Valley in Africa—a 2,100-mile (3,360-km) gash through eastern Africa from Mozambique to Ethiopia. The Red Sea and Gulf of Aden in the Middle East were also formed by plates spreading apart.

At convergent plate boundaries, plates move toward one another. When they meet, there is a collision that occurs in slow motion, and something has to give. Sometimes the edge of one plate sinks under the edge of another. This usually

DIVERGENT

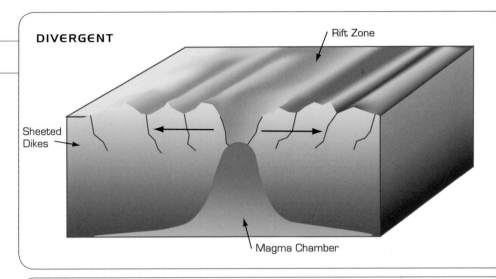

Rift Zone

Sheeted Dikes

Magma Chamber

CONVERGENT

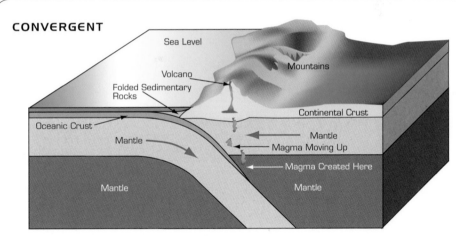

Sea Level

Mountains

Volcano

Folded Sedimentary Rocks

Oceanic Crust

Continental Crust

Mantle

Mantle

Magma Moving Up

Magma Created Here

Mantle

Mantle

TRANSFORM

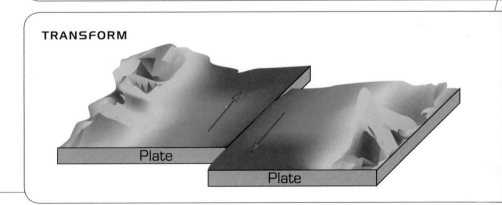

Plate

Plate

occurs when a heavier plate meets a lighter plate, such as when plates carrying continents meet plates carrying the sea-floor. This sinking is called subduction.

As the edge of a heavier seafloor plate sinks downward under a lighter continental plate or another seafloor plate, it begins to melt in the high temperature of the mantle. Geologists say this has the effect of recycling Earth's crust. At other places where both plates carry continents, the edge of one plate crumples up against the other to form mountains. The Himalayas, the highest mountain range in the world, is still forming in a head-on collision between the Indo-Australian plate and the Eurasian plate.

The beautiful Lake Manyara National Park in Tanzania is part of the Great Rift Valley.

In other places where plates meet, they neither collide nor pull apart—they slide past one another. These places are called transform plate boundaries. At transform boundaries, no new crust is formed and no existing crust is lost. The Pacific plate and the North American plate are sliding past one another near the coast of California.

All plate boundaries are prone to earthquakes. The earthquakes at convergent and transform boundaries can be especially dangerous.

The Nanga Parbat mountain is the ninth highest peak in the world and is located at the western end of the Great Himalayan mountain range.

Plates and Earthquakes

The motion of Earth's tectonic plates can set off earthquakes in areas that contain faults, which are fractures or weak places in blocks of rock. Faults usually occur along plate boundaries. The melting of a plate edge as it subducts under another plate can also set off a series of events that trigger earthquakes. Geologists, however, have found some faults in the middle of huge plates.

FAULTS AND FAULT MOVEMENTS

Just as tectonic plates move relative to one another, so does the rock on either side of a fault. There are three types of faults: strike-slip, normal, and reverse. Some faults are visible on the ground. Most faults, however, are deep within the crust.

Each fault can occur at any type of boundary. The main type of fault along transform boundaries are strike-slip faults. In a strike-slip fault, the blocks of rock move sideways as they pass each other. As the huge plates grind past one another, the force pulls on the rocks of nearby faults. Sometimes the rocks along these fault edges get stuck together. As the plates keep moving, stress builds up along the fault. Suddenly, the rocks break free and the edges of the fault move. The sudden movement sets off an earthquake.

Normal faults usually occur at divergent boundaries, such as areas where sections of the seafloor are spreading apart and new crust is forming. Normal

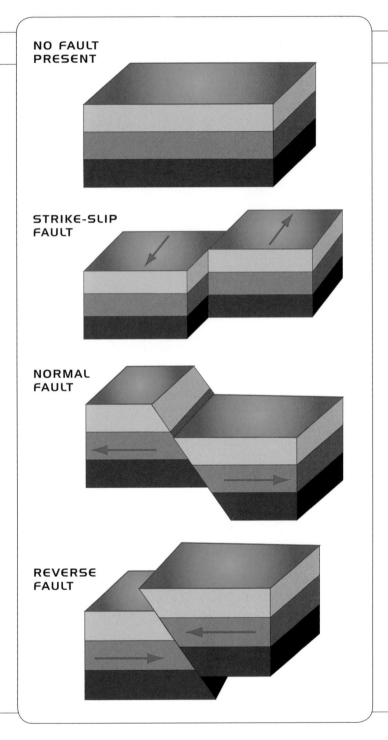

NO FAULT
PRESENT

STRIKE-SLIP
FAULT

NORMAL
FAULT

REVERSE
FAULT

faults result from tremendous stress when the rock on one side moves downward against the rock on the other side.

Reverse faults result from compressional forces and typically occur where two plates are coming together. Reverse faulting is just the opposite of normal faulting. The rock on one side of the fault moves upward, rising above the rock on the other side. These movements set off earthquakes.

The severity of an earthquake depends upon the size of the break in a fault. The farther the crack travels, the more severe the quake will be. The crack can travel at high speed. A fault fracture in granite, for example, travels at about 2 miles (3 km) per second.

A fault scarp, which is a cliff or slope formed from movement along a fault, can be seen in the desert near Landers, California.

Earthquakes Around the World

Most earthquakes in the United States occur along the West Coast from California to Alaska, where the Pacific, North American, and smaller plates are grinding past one another. In 1906, a great earthquake almost destroyed the city of San Francisco. In 1964, an even more powerful earthquake struck southern Alaska.

Other powerful earthquakes occurred in the middle of the North American plate. For a three-month period between 1811 and 1812, the area around New Madrid, Missouri, was struck by a series of four earthquakes that could be felt from southern Canada to the Gulf of Mexico and from the Atlantic coast to the Rocky Mountains. The New Madrid earthquakes were powerful enough to destroy forests and change the course of the Mississippi River.

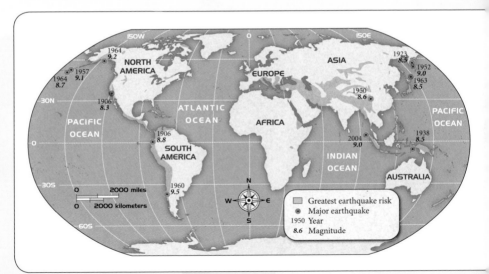

Earthquakes can occur all over the world.

WAVES IN ROCK

Earthquakes cause damage to buildings and other structures because earthquake waves travel through the crust. The waves begin at the focus, the point along the fault where the break begins. The focus can be deep underground. The point on the surface above the focus is called the epicenter. The waves are strongest near the epicenter, which is where the most damage occurs.

There are two types of seismic waves, or earthquake waves: body waves and surface waves. Body waves travel deep through Earth's interior, while surface waves ripple along Earth's surface.

There are two kinds of body waves: compressional and shear. Compressional body waves move through rock much as sound waves move through air. They compress or push on the rock as they pass through, creating a push-pull effect that makes the rock move back and forth. Compres-

A 1994 earthquake caused two sections of a bridge in Los Angeles to collapse.

BODY WAVES travel deep under the ground. There are two types:

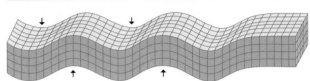

COMPRESSION   EXPANSION   COMPRESSION

P waves push and pull on the ground, moving particles together and apart.

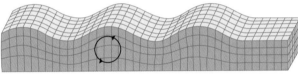

S waves move the ground up and down and from side to side.

SURFACE WAVES can only move along the surface of the ground. There are two types:

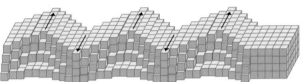

Rayleigh waves roll along the ground, moving particles in circles.

Love waves move the ground from side to side.

sional waves are also called P waves, or primary waves. Shear body waves snake through the rock, making it move from side to side and up and down. Shear waves, also called S waves, are the seismic waves that cause the most damage. Geologists study seismic body waves passing through Earth to learn about the layers of Earth.

There are also two kinds of surface waves: Love and Rayleigh. Rayleigh waves are more like water waves, causing the ground to roll as the waves pass by. Love waves move horizontally, causing the surface of the ground to move from side to side.

Earthquakes can cause enormous waves in the ocean. Undersea earthquakes can cause undersea landslides, which in turn can trigger a gigantic wave on the ocean surface called a tsunami. Tsunamis are often undetected until they come close to a shore because the height of the wave is only a few feet in deep water. As the water becomes shallower, the wave piles up. Tsunamis can tower as high as 100 feet (30 meters) as they crash onto the shore. A series of tsunamis triggered by an earthquake under the Indian Ocean killed about 230,000 people in Thailand, Indonesia, and other Southeast Asian countries on December 26, 2004.

DID YOU KNOW?

Following an earthquake, the first waves seismographs detect are P waves, because these waves travel faster than other seismic waves.

Forceful waves of a tsunami in Sri Lanka threw fishing boats onto land.

Plates and Volcanoes

GEOLOGISTS DEFINE VOLCANOES as more than just fountains of fiery lava shooting out of a mountaintop. Any vent, or opening, in Earth's crust is a volcano if magma or material heated by magma pours out of it. Volcanic vents can give off gases, hot water, and tephra (volcanic dust, ash, or boulders). Magma oozes up out of vents along the Mid-Atlantic Ridge to form lava. Red-hot lava flows in rivers down the sides of volcanoes in Hawaii. The side of Mount St. Helens in the Cascade Range blew off in 1980, burying the surrounding lakes and forests in a thick blanket of hot ash. Most volcanic eruptions are caused by shifting tectonic plates. Certain plate move-

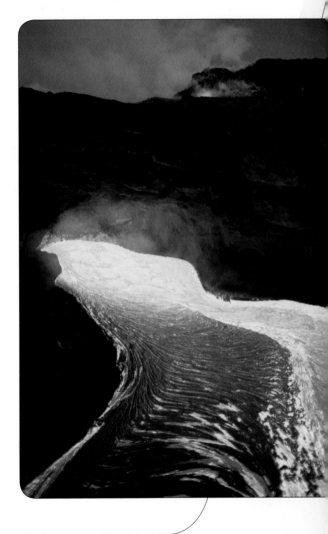

A river of lava exploded out of an opening and flowed down the side of a volcano.

COMPOSITE

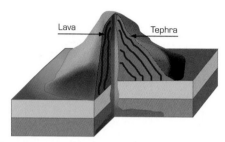

Composite volcanoes are made from a buildup of alternating layers of lava and tephra.

CINDER CONE

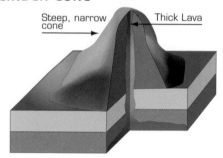

Cinder cone volcanoes are made from tephra that explodes out of a vent.

SHIELD

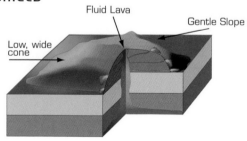

Shield volcanoes are created when lava erupts from tubes within the volcano. The lava then hardens, creating a layer of rock over the volcano.

ments are responsible for different kinds of volcanic eruptions.

SUBDUCTION AND MOUNT ST. HELENS

Until May 1980, the scene around snow-capped Mount St. Helens in Washington state was one of exquisite beauty and tranquility. The still surface of Spirit Lake at the base of the mountain reflected the blue sky and the surrounding green spires of ancient evergreen trees. Then, with a rumbling that grew to a roar, the side of the mountain was blown away by a huge volcanic eruption. The force of the explosion knocked over giant trees as if they were

toothpicks. Tephra turned lovely Spirit Lake into an ugly gray pond. The heat of the eruption melted snow on the mountain, which caused rivers of mud to pour down the mountainsides.

Volcanologists were not surprised. They had been monitoring the warning signs, such as steam and earthquakes, for months. Then in April they noticed a bulge growing on the side of the mountain. This was a sign that pressure from hot gases and rising magma was building up inside the volcano. They warned everyone to stay away, and all but 57 people escaped the blast.

The chain of events that led to the eruption of Mount St. Helens began with the melting of the edge of the Juan de Fuca plate. The edge of the heavier Juan de Fuca plate was pulled downward as it met the lighter North American plate. The

Volcanic ash burst out of Mount St. Helens in 1980.

edge of the Juan de Fuca plate melted in the high temperatures of the asthenosphere. At this point, the melting plate edge was under the western part of the North American plate.

The melting caused magma to build up. In places, the magma formed underground pools of molten rock, called magma chambers. Some magma worked its way up to the surface by melting a channel through weak parts in the rock above. As rock was melted by the rising magma, the rock released hot gases. Eventually, the magma erupted from a vent in the ground above to create the volcanic Mount St. Helens. In the same way, volcanoes form all around the Ring of Fire.

DID YOU KNOW?

In the 1700s, some people thought the red-hot lava that erupted from volcanoes was caused by burning underground deposits of coal.

Small spurts erupted from a large pool of lava.

Ring of Fire

Earthquakes frequently shake the crust around the Pacific Ocean, from the west coasts of South and North America to the eastern edges of Asia. About 350 active volcanoes—more than half of all the active volcanoes on Earth—are located around this Pacific Rim. Because there is so much volcanic activity, the area is called the Ring of Fire.

The Ring of Fire lies along the edges of the enormous Pacific Ocean. The Pacific plate is being squeezed as the seafloor spreads out from the middle of the Atlantic and eastern Pacific oceans. As a result, the edges of the Pacific plate are being forced down into the mantle by subduction. The friction across the plate boundaries sets off earthquakes. Heat from the mantle below melts the lava that erupts violently from volcanoes.

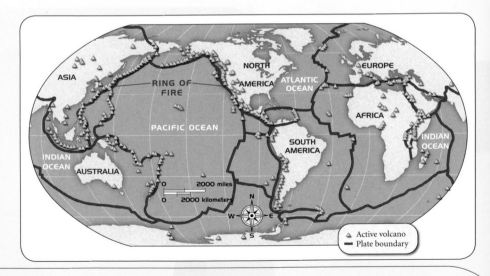

Many of the world's volcanoes are located along the Ring of Fire.

DIVERGENCE AND ICELAND'S GEYSERS

Hot springs bubble, geysers spout fountains of steaming hot water high into the air, and lava flows out of deep cracks along the rugged, rocky center of Iceland, an island nation in the North Atlantic Ocean. Iceland has geysers, hot springs, and more than 200 volcanoes because part of the island sits on the North American plate and part of it sits on the Eurasian plate. As these plates move away from each other, Iceland is torn down its center, causing the two sections to move apart as well. Between the moving plates, magma rises from the asthenosphere below, providing molten rock for the volcanoes and heat for the geysers and hot springs.

Yellowstone National Park's Old Faithful, one of the most famous geysers in the world, shoots water that is heated and pressurized by magma deep underground.

The same processes responsible for Iceland's volcanoes created the underwater mountain range called the Mid-Atlantic Ridge. The Mid-Atlantic Ridge is part of a large system of underwater mountains that encircles Earth. As the North American and Eurasian plates slowly spread apart, magma oozes up through cracks in the seafloor called fissures. The lava that flows out creates new seafloor and builds up ridges that can become mountains. Some of the mountains grow so tall that they rise above the ocean surface. The tops of some of these mountains became islands, such as Iceland, Ascension Island, and the Azores.

Islands are created from the tops of undersea volcanic mountains, such as Surtsey Island in Iceland.

HAWAIIAN HOT SPOT

Not all volcanic islands are formed at plate boundaries. The Hawaiian Islands, for example, were formed by a different process. Hawaii sits in the middle of the Pacific plate. Geologists believe there is a very hot spot in the mantle deep under the Pacific plate. Like a blowtorch, hot magma blasts through the lithosphere as the Pacific plate slowly moves to the northwest. Geologists are still not sure what hot spots are, what causes them, or whether or not they move around.

Over millions of years, lava from the undersea Hawaiian volcanoes built up. As the Pacific plate moved over the hot spot, new islands formed. Hawaii actually consists of more than 130 islands, though only seven islands are inhabited. The other islands are tiny bits of rock and atolls, which are rings of coral on the tops of sunken volcanoes. Many of these volcanic mountaintops were eroded by wind and ocean waves and are barely visible.

Most of the Hawaiian volcanoes became dormant after that

DID YOU KNOW?

The world's largest volcano is Mauna Loa, which rises 13,770 feet (4,200 meters) above sea level on the island of Hawaii. Part of Mauna Loa, however, extends 15,840 feet (4,831 m) under the ocean.

section of the Pacific plate moved away from the hot spot. Two volcanoes on the big island of Hawaii are still active, Mauna Loa and Kilauea. Mauna Loa, the world's largest volcano, last erupted in 1984. Lava flows almost constantly from Kilauea, where the U.S. Geological Survey has a volcano laboratory.

Geologists from the Hawaiian Volcano Observatory monitored a river of lava flowing from Kilauea.

The oldest inhabitable Hawaiian islands are Niihau and Kauai in the northwest. The youngest is Hawaii, which is still over the hot spot. The hot spot is forming another Hawaiian island, Loihi, a volcanic mountain about 22 miles (35 km) southeast of the island of Hawaii. Loihi is now 2 miles (3 km) above the seafloor and less than $\frac{6}{10}$ mile (1 km) below the surface of the ocean.

The state of Hawaii is composed of many volcanic islands.

Studying Plate Tectonics ⊕

THE THEORY OF PLATE TECTONICS is one of the newest scientific concepts. Although the idea that the continents were not always in the same place was first suggested in the 1500s, it was not until about 1912 that any scientist took it seriously.

That year, a German meteorologist named Alfred Lothar Wegener began to give lectures about his theory of continental drift. According to this theory, all the land on Earth was once part of a supercontinent called Pangaea. While some scientists believe there may have been pre-existing supercontinents, Wegener believed Pangaea began to break apart into two large continents: Laurasia in the Northern Hemisphere and Gondwana in the Southern Hemisphere. These two huge continents continued to break up and move apart, eventually forming the landmasses that exist today.

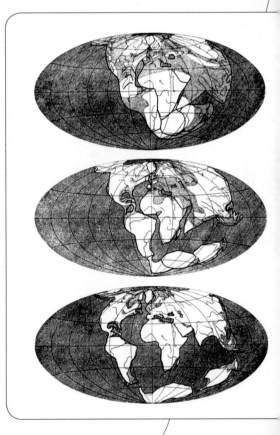

The continents have drifted far away from their positions in Pangaea millions of years ago.

Alfred Lothar Wegener

Alfred Lothar Wegener was born on November 1, 1880, in Berlin, Germany, and was educated as a planetary astronomer. He became interested in meteorology and many other branches of science. He began to wonder why the coastlines of Africa and South America seemed to fit together like puzzle pieces.

In 1914, while serving in the German army at the beginning of World War I, he was injured and sent to a hospital. While he was recovering, he realized that various branches of science, including the study of rocks and fossils, would be needed to figure out the mystery of the shapes of continents.

In 1915, he published a book called *The Origin of Continents and Oceans*, which detailed his theory of continental drift. Few scientists thought this theory was valid.

Wegener went to Greenland several times to conduct meteorological studies before becoming a professor of meteorology and geophysics in Austria. In November 1930, Wegener died during a winter storm while returning from a mission to deliver supplies to other meteorologists in Greenland.

Alfred Wegener's continental drift theory is still used by scientists today.

Few scientists supported the theory of continental drift. How could the huge continents plow through the dense rocks on the ocean floor? Wegener was never able to provide a good answer.

FOSSIL EVIDENCE

Although he could not explain how the continents moved, Wegener believed he had firm evidence that they did move. He pointed out that fossils of the same ancient plants and animals

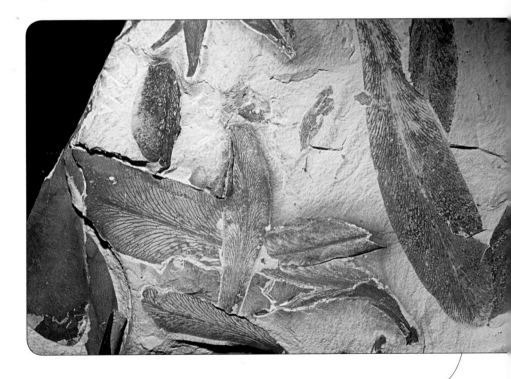

The fossils of leaves from the glossopteris tree were found on different continents.

are found on the facing coasts of Africa and South America, which have similar shapes. There was no way the animals could have swum across the Atlantic Ocean. And how could the plants have gotten there?

In addition, the climates on certain continents had changed radically from ancient times. For example, there are coal deposits on the frozen continent of Antarctica. Since coal is formed from vegetation in tropical swamps, Wegener believed this indicated that Antarctica was once close to the equator.

SEAFLOOR MAPPING

Scientists began to get a good idea of what the seafloor looked like in the early 1900s. They bounced sound waves off the ocean bottom and measured how long it took them to return. These echo soundings provided evidence that there were mountains on some parts of the seafloor, particularly in the middle of the Atlantic Ocean. By the late 1950s, geologists knew that an underwater mountain range went around the planet. They called it the global mid-ocean ridge.

Soon afterward, in the 1960s, oceanographers learned that magnetic minerals in seafloor rocks formed unusual magnetic stripes on either side of the mid-ocean ridge. Volcanic rocks contain a natural magnetic mineral called magnetite that lines up in the direction of Earth's magnetic field. In the past, when

the molten rock hardened, the grains of magnetite were "frozen" in place, preserving a record of Earth's ancient magnetism. Because Earth's magnetic field reversed itself many times

Although the seafloor in ice caves can easily be studied by scientists, advanced equipment is needed to map the parts of the ocean floor at greater depths.

in the past, sometimes the magnetite in the rock pointed north and other times south. As new crust formed at the mid-ocean ridge, the rocks preserved the orientation of Earth's magnetic field at that time. The magnetically striped rock pattern indicated that over millions of years, new crust formed along the ridge.

Geologists also learned that some of the crust beneath the ocean is much younger than they had thought. Some scientists began to suspect that Wegener was right. They theorized that the ocean crust was separating at the mid-ocean ridge. They called this theory seafloor spreading.

Traces of magnetite in the ocean indicate the patterns of ancient magnetic fields of Earth.

GLOMAR CHALLENGER

In 1968, a major earth science project, the Deep Sea Drilling Project, began operating a drill ship called *Glomar Challenger* that was used for deep-sea research. This ship drilled cores of sediment and rock along the Mid-Atlantic Ridge. Geologists determined the ages of these samples and found that

The *Glomar Challenger* provided scientists with a better analysis of the Mid-Atlantic Ridge.

rocks nearest the middle of the ridge were the youngest. The farther from the ridge, the older the rocks were. Furthermore, these increasing ages matched those predicted by the magnetic stripes. Samples drilled by *Glomar Challenger*, and later by another drill ship called *JOIDES Resolution*, strongly supported the theory of seafloor spreading.

COMPLETING THE THEORY

If new crust was forming, where was the old crust going? Geologists found deep undersea trenches beneath the edges of the Pacific plate. They concluded that the crust was somehow being recycled back into the mantle along these deep trenches. Studies using seismic waves showed that most earthquakes take place along or near ridges, trenches, or transform faults. Scientists also used seismic wave studies to learn more about the interior of Earth. Altogether, these studies supported the theory of plate tectonics.

WHY PLATES MOVE

Ultimately, plate motion is driven by the release of heat from deep in the Earth's interior. Geologists first believed that currents within the hot mantle drove the movement of the plates. Now they believe that gravity is the force responsible for specific plate movements. For example, a floating washcloth will stay on the surface of the water until one of its edges is submerged. Then the rest of the washcloth is sucked underneath at an increasing rate. In the same sense, gravity pulls the denser rock at the edge of a plate down into the asthenosphere in areas where subduction is common. This type of movement is called slab-pull.

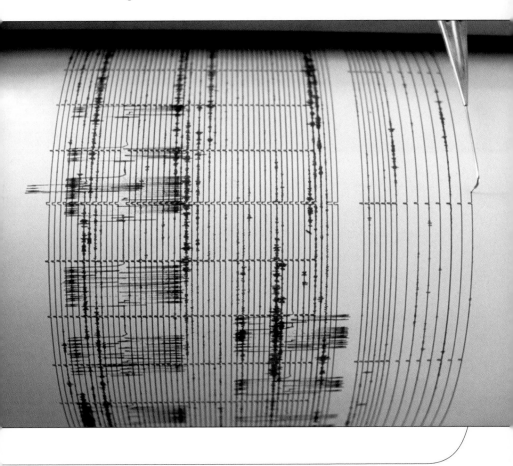

The differences between the line intensities on a seismograph, which represent seismic waves, indicate the severity of an earthquake.

Geologists also believe that at the point where plates sepa-rate, gravity pulls plates downhill away from mid-ocean ridges where new crust forms. They call this force ridge-push. Over-all, plates move at rates of between 1 and 10 inches (2.5 to 25 cm) per year.

The theory of plate tectonics gave geologists a logical way to explain the workings of Earth and its layers. They are using their knowledge in many ways. For example, geologists can better predict earthquakes and volcanic eruptions. Meanwhile, geologists use advanced technology to continue learning about Earth's fascinating surface and how it moves.

A volcanologist collected samples of lava for analysis.

asthenosphere—layer of soft, hot rock below the lithosphere

body waves—seismic waves that travel through Earth

convergent boundaries—plate boundaries that come together

core—innermost layer of Earth

crust—Earth's thin outer layer of rock

divergent boundaries—plate boundaries that move apart

epicenter—point on the ground above the focus of an earthquake

faults—breaks in the rock of Earth's crust

fissures—cracks in the crust, usually in the seafloor

focus—point in a fault where an earthquake begins

fossils—hardened remains or imprints of ancient organisms

geysers—springs that shoot hot water or steam into the air

hot spot—a region of very hot magma in the mantle

lava—magma that reaches Earth's surface and erupts from a volcano

lithosphere—Earth's crust and the upper part of the mantle

magma—molten rock beneath Earth's crust

mantle—layer of hot rock between Earth's crust and core

plate boundaries—edges of tectonic plates

seismic waves—waves created by an earthquake

seismographs—machines for detecting the strength and direction of earthquakes or other movements in Earth's crust

subduction—the sinking of one plate edge beneath another

surface waves—seismic waves that travel along the surface of Earth

tectonic plates—slabs of Earth's crust that move about on a layer of molten rock

tephra—volcanic rocks, dust, and ash

transform boundaries—plate boundaries that move past one another

tsunami—gigantic ocean wave created by an undersea earthquake, landslide, or volcanic eruption

▸ Tectonic plates, like other features on Earth, can change or even disappear. Some plates, such as the Juan de Fuca plate, get smaller. This plate off the coast of Oregon and Washington was once part of the larger Farallon plate, which broke up. The Juan de Fuca plate will someday be subducted under the North American plate and disappear.

▸ Iceland is splitting apart. The Mid-Atlantic Ridge, where the seafloor is spreading and new crust is forming, runs right through the island nation. Many earth scientists use Iceland as a natural laboratory in which to study tectonic plates.

▸ The earthquake that set off deadly tsunamis in Southeast Asia in December 2004 was the largest since the Alaska earthquake of 1964. The tsunamis left about 230,000 people dead, with 128,000 of them classified as missing. Officials believe the number of deaths will never be known.

▸ The largest fragments of tephra are called volcanic bombs.

▸ The deepest known part of the ocean lies in the Mariana Trench, an area southeast of Guam, where the Pacific plate is undergoing subduction. The bottom is 36,198 feet (11,040 m) below the surface of the Pacific Ocean.

▸ Visitors to Yellowstone National Park in the western United States see fountains of hot water shooting out of geysers and pools of bubbling hot mud. Hot rocks underneath the park provide energy for these natural wonders. Yellowstone is not near the edge of a tectonic plate, so geologists believe the heat comes from a hot spot under the North American plate. Evidence of large volcanic craters in the park also leads geologists to believe that Yellowstone was once the site of a supervolcano.

▸ The world's deepest lake, Lake Baikal in Russia, contains as much freshwater as all of the Great Lakes. It was created by the movement of tectonic plates and is located in a break in one of the most complex fault zones in the world.

Lake Baikal, Russia

At the Library

Edwards, John. *Plate Tectonics and Continental Drift.* North Mankato, Minn: Smart Apple Media, 2006.

Harrison, David L. *Mountains: The Tops of the World.* Honesdale, Pa: Boyds Mills Press, 2005.

Hooper, Meredith. *The Island That Moved: How Shifting Forces Shape Our Earth.* New York: Viking, 2004.

Johnson, Rebecca L. *Plate Tectonics.* Minneapolis: Lerner Publishing Group, 2005.

On the Web

For more information on this topic, use FactHound.
1. Go to *www.facthound.com*
2. Type in this book ID: **0756519578**
3. Click on the *Fetch It* button.

FactHound will find the best Web sites for you.

On the Road

Hawaii Volcanoes National Park
P.O. Box 52
Hawaii National Park, HI
96718-0052
808/985-6000

Museum of Science
Science Park
Boston, MA 02114
617/589-0100

Explore all the Earth Science books

Erosion: How Land Forms, How It Changes
ISBN: 0-7565-0854-1

Natural Resources: Using and Protecting Earth's Supplies
ISBN: 0-7565-0856-8

The Greenhouse Effect: Warming the Planet
ISBN: 0-7565-1956-X

Plate Tectonics: Earth's Moving Crust
ISBN: 0-7565-1957-8

Minerals: From Apatite to Zinc
ISBN: 0-7565-0855-X

Soil: Digging Into Earth's Vital Resource
ISBN: 0-7565-0857-6

A complete list of Exploring Science titles is available on our Web site: *www.compasspointbooks.com*